Are you ready to embark on a thrilling adventure with Dotty, a little girl with special eyes, and her incredible imaginary friend, Mr. Fuzzywuggle? Join them as they explore the magnificent world of the zoo and interact with the most fantastic animals you can imagine. From surprises to magical encounters, this enchanting tale will fill you with joy, warmth, and inspiration. Your imagination will soar as you experience the wonder and excitement of the zoo alongside Dotty and Mr. Fuzzywuggle. Don't miss out on this incredible journey!

Dedication Page

"This book is lovingly dedicated to my incredible husband and children. You constantly inspire and support me, bringing boundless joy to my life and motivating me to strive for greatness. My love for you knows no bounds. I love you all to the moon and back."

Dotty woke up to find her imaginary friend, Mr. Fuzzywuggle, nudging her and whispering, "Wake up." Mr. Fuzzywuggle was an extraordinary creature with soft green fur that felt like freshly mowed grass. He had a large, red, heart-shaped button on his tummy that shone brightly in the sunlight and possessed magical powers. One of his eyes was green, while the other was brown and sparkled with mischief. His nose was round and large, and his teeth were big and white, revealing a friendly smile. He had big, pointy ears that twitched whenever he heard a new sound. And the best part? Mr. Fuzzywuggle always smelled like sweet strawberries.

Dotty woke up, stretched, and yawned. She opened her big green eyes and pushed her long brown hair away from her face. Her cheeks looked pink and rosy from being warm and cosy in her bed. Dotty sat up with a huge smile, ready for an adventure.

Dotty and Mr. Fuzzywuggle were the best of friends! They loved spending time together and always found ways to have fun. Mr. Fuzzywuggle was a playful little fellow who would jump on the bed with Dotty and make her laugh until her sides hurt. They went on adventures together and always had a fantastic time together.

"Once owned by a little girl, Mr. Fuzzywuggle was left behind as she grew older. However, he has now found a new friend in Dotty. Mr. Fuzzywuggle has been an imaginary friend to many children, taking them on exciting adventures across all five continents - Africa, Asia, Australia, North America, and South America. He has even led children on exciting adventures, from the top of the Pyramids in Egypt to exploring outer space."

"Let's go on an adventure!" squealed Dotty, her eyes twinkling with excitement. "How about we visit the zoo?" Mr. Fuzzywuggle's furry face lit up with joy, and he replied, "Absolutely!" They held hands and with a magical tap of Dotty's sparkling red Cane, Mr. Fuzzywuggle's heart glowed with wonder. They soared into the air, feeling the wind rush past their faces, and the exhilaration of the unknown ahead. The sweet scent of fresh strawberries filled the air, and they eagerly anticipated the wild and unforgettable journey to the Zoo.

Dotty and Mr. Fuzzywuggle were thrilled as they reached the bustling zoo. The sound of lions roaring and birds singing made Mr. Fuzzywuggle's ears twitch with excitement. As they strolled through the zoo, they suddenly caught a disgusting smell. They pinched their noses and asked each other, "What's that smell?" Mr. Fuzzywuggle realised that they were standing near a big pile of hippopotamus poop. "Yuck!" Mr. Fuzzywuggle exclaimed as he grabbed Dotty's hand and hurried away while Dotty giggled at his reaction.

Dotty's heart raced as she heard strange noises around her, causing her to feel frightened. She couldn't help but cry. Mr. Fuzzywuggle noticed her distress and reached out to gently take her hand, offering comfort. "I'm sorry you're feeling scared, Dotty. I know it's tough, but don't worry. I'm here for you, and I'll keep you safe. It's okay to feel scared sometimes; we all do. Take a deep breath and remember, everything will be alright. We'll get through this together, okay?" Dotty sniffled and cuddled into Mr. Fuzzywuggle for comfort.

Mr. Fuzzywuggle came up with a brilliant idea to help Dotty overcome her fear. He asked her, "Can you hear the 'ooo ooo' sound?" Dotty, trembling, replied, "Yes." Mr. Fuzzywuggle explained to her that this was the sound of monkeys having fun. He then showed her that they could watch the monkeys from behind the glass, but the monkeys could not reach them because there was a barrier between them. He placed Dotty's hand on the glass to help her understand that she could overcome her fear and enjoy their adventure. Dotty smiled and had fun with Mr. Fuzzywuggle, watching the naughty monkeys.

As Dotty and Mr. Fuzzywuggle wandered around the zoo, they heard a loud noise that frightened Dotty. She screamed, "I'm scared!" and tightly held Mr. Fuzzywuggle's hand. She asked him what it could be. As they moved closer, they heard a roar. Dotty realised it was the sound of lions. She clung onto Mr. Fuzzywuggle's hand even tighter as they continued walking. Suddenly, they heard a very sad crying noise. The sound became louder as they turned the corner, but it suddenly stopped. Mr. Fuzzywuggle pulled Dotty closer and said, "Dotty! Dotty! It's an..." elephant!"

"Oh... hello," said the elephant in a sad voice. Dotty was surprised to hear the elephant talking and asked for her name. "My name is Bonnie," she sniffled. "Hello, my name is Dotty, and this is Mr. Fuzzywuggle," replied Dotty. "Why are you so sad?" Dotty asked Bonnie.

Mr. Fuzzywuggle whispered something in Dotty's ear, and she smiled, "Yes, what a great idea!" Bonnie looked puzzled but excited. Dotty and Mr. Fuzzywuggle held hands and exchanged a glance. Dotty tapped her Cane on the floor, causing it to sparkle brightly in red. Mr. Fuzzywuggle's heart began to glow red as well. Soon after, the two floated over the fence and landed beside Bonnie, who was surprised by their sudden appearance.

Bonnie suddenly sneezed, causing Dotty and Mr. Fuzzywuggle to jump in surprise. "Well, you see," explained Bonnie, "I have caught a cold and can't stop sneezing. I have sneezed so much that I now have a knot in my trunk, and it hurts." Achoo! Bonnie sneezed once again.

Achooooo!

"Oh, you poor thing," said Dotty, trying to comfort Bonnie. Meanwhile, Mr. Fuzzywuggle, a jolly and playful creature, pranced around Bonnie and started blowing bubbles out of his ears to make her smile. Bonnie couldn't resist the sight of the bubbles and finally burst into laughter. Dotty and Mr. Fuzzywuggle were pleased that they could ease Bonnie's worries and brighten her day."

Bonnie noticed that Dotty was holding a long cane and became curious. Dotty explained that she was blind from birth and used the Cane to "see" the ground and avoid bumping into things. When Bonnie asked Dotty how it felt to be blind, Dotty shared that she has special eyes and sees the world differently. Despite being blind, Dotty was brave and strong in finding her way around. Bonnie was impressed and inspired by Dotty's story.

Dotty was eager to find out what Bonnie looked like. According to Mr. Fuzzywuggle, Bonnie had a big body, big flappy ears, big round squishy feet, a long trunk, and big teeth. But Bonnie kindly pointed out to Mr. Fuzzywuggle that they were tusks, not teeth, which got everyone laughing.

Dotty reached out to touch Bonnie's trunk but was startled by her cry of pain. "Oh, I'm so sorry," Dotty said. "I didn't mean to hurt you." "Perhaps you can use your Cane to untie the knot in Bonnie's trunk," suggested Mr Fuzzywuggle. "Can I?" asked Dotty, unsure of her abilities. "Absolutely," replied Mr Fuzzywuggle with a reassuring smile. Dotty took Mr Fuzzywuggle's hand and tapped her Cane three times. The Cane began to glow red, and Mr Fuzzywuggle's heart glowed. Suddenly, Bonnie's trunk was untangled. "Thank you so much," said Bonnie gratefully as she took a long drink of water. "That's much better."

Bonnie thanked Dotty and Mr Fuzzywuggle for their kindness and offered them a ride on her back to show her appreciation. Excitedly, they climbed on board, holding on tightly as Bonnie effortlessly leapt over the fence with her strong muscles. Bonnie confidently led the way as they continued to explore.

Bonnie and her two best friends, Dotty and Mr. Fuzzywuggle, were running through the zoo, filled with excitement. Suddenly, they stumbled upon Kasey the Koala, perched high on a tree. Kasey was surprised by their sudden appearance and almost fell from her branch! Just then, Albie, the menacing alligator, jumped at them with a fierce snap, sending shivers down their spines. Unaware of the danger they had just escaped, Bonnie and her friends continued their wild adventure, not realising that Albie had almost bitten his tail!

As they passed by Pedro the Penguin, who was enjoying his fishy meal, they greeted him with a friendly "Hi!" Pedro was shocked by Bonnie's sudden appearance, and to his surprise, he waved back, accidentally dropping his fish. Further along their journey, they encountered Gerald the Giraffe, munching on leaves from a nearby tree. As Bonnie zoomed by, Gerald was so amazed that he dropped his food and stretched his long neck to watch Bonnie disappear into the distance.

Dotty was exhausted and let out a massive yawn, which made Bonnie realise it was time to head back. The two friends slid down Bonnie's enormous trunk, shrieking with delight. They had an exciting adventure at the Zoo with Bonnie, and she was thankful to them for making her trunk feel better. As they said their goodbyes, Dotty and Mr Fuzzywuggle kissed Bonnie and held hands while banging the Cane three times. Suddenly, the Cane erupted into a brilliant red, and Mr.Fuzzywuggle's heart began to glow. With one last shout to Bonnie, they flew into the air with a whoosh.

Dotty settled into her cosy bed and tightly squeezed Mr. Fuzzywuggle. She whispered a sweet goodnight, to which Mr. Fuzzywuggle replied, "Goodnight, Dotty! Have sweet dreams." Dotty's heart felt warm and fuzzy as she closed her eyes and drifted off to sleep, thinking about her next adventure with Mr.Fuzzywuggle. Would it be a tea party with her favourite toys, exploring outer space, or diving into the ocean for a wondrous journey? Dotty warmly invites you to join her on these exciting adventures. So, hold on tight for the next one!

Printed in Great Britain
by Amazon

44003971R00027